Simple Steps to Help You
Shopping Addicti

By

Colvin Tonya Nyakundi

Mendon Cottage Books

JD-Biz Publishing

All Rights Reserved.

No part of this publication may be reproduced in any form or by any means, including scanning, photocopying, or otherwise without prior written permission from JD-Biz Corp Copyright © 2015

All Images Licensed by Fotolia and 123RF.

Disclaimer

The information is this book is provided for informational purposes only. It is not intended to be used and medical advice or a substitute for proper medical treatment by a qualified health care provider. The information is believed to be accurate as presented based on research by the author.

The contents have not been evaluated by the U.S. Food and Drug Administration or any other Government or Health Organization and the contents in this book are not to be used to treat cure or prevent disease.

The author or publisher is not responsible for the use or safety of any diet, procedure or treatment mentioned in this book. The author or publisher is not responsible for errors or omissions that may exist.

Warning

The Book is for informational purposes only and before taking on any diet, treatment or medical procedure, it is recommended to consult with your primary health care provider.

Our books are available at

1. Amazon.com
2. Barnes and Noble
3. Itunes
4. Kobo
5. Smashwords
6. Google Play Books

Table of Contents

Introduction 3
What is Shopping Addiction? 4
How Do You Know if You Are a Shopping Addict? 7
How Shopping Addiction is affecting Your Life Negatively 13
What Can You Do to Overcome Addiction to shopping? 18
How to Ensure You Won't Ever Become a Shopping Addict Again 26
Conclusion 29
Author Bio 30
Publisher 41

Introduction

Just like in many other parts of the world, there are millions of people in the United States addicted to shopping. However, very few people know or admit that they have this problem and therefore need help. Addiction to shopping is a universal problem that can affect anybody regardless of their financial status, age, gender or current location.

Some people are so much addicted to shopping that they forget their other obligations. When addicted to shopping you could spend huge portions of your income on shopping while ignoring other important financial commitments such as your child's fees, medical insurance and utility bills. If you are a shopping addict, you don't need to worry about anything because you can easily stop the addiction after reading this book.

Countless people have managed to stop their addiction to shopping by implementing the simple steps in this book. After reading the book, you'll be in a position to help other people overcome their shopping addiction problem. You also get important tips on how to ensure that you won't ever become a shopping addict again.

Start the process of overcoming your shopping addiction by reading the book "Simple Steps to Help You Overcome Shopping Addiction!!!"

What is Shopping Addiction?

(young woman walking in the street after shopping)

When you hear the word 'addiction', what comes to your mind? Addiction is a word that is highly associated with the abuse of drugs and other controlled substances including alcohol, cigarettes, heroin, cocaine and meth. Some people even think that you can only get addicted to something that you ingest into your body. Shopping addiction is a condition in which the shopping addict has an abnormal desire to purchase something. People having this problem tend to purchase goods uncontrollably without giving it a second thought.

Addiction to shopping is a problem that affects millions of people around the world. When addicted to shopping, you'll find yourself buying something simply because you saw it on display. You can even spend the money that was meant to be used elsewhere. One common character in shopping addicts is that they purchase products impulsively and like making payments online, through credit cards or debit cards.

When making payments via credit cards, debit cards or online, they think that they are not actually paying for the product. However, the truth of the matter is that you'll be spending your money regardless of your payment option. You therefore have to be very careful when purchasing products that you have not budgeted for.

When walking along the street, have you ever felt that you must purchase a given pair of shoe or even shirt simply because you saw it on display? When browsing on your computer, have you ever purchased something that you had not budgeted for? Maybe you saw an advert and then decided to purchase the product online? Well, if your answer is 'yes' to any of the above books, that could be an indication that you are addicted to shopping. You can be addicted to shopping over the internet, when visiting the local department store, at the mall or even when traveling.

Some of the commodities that shopping addicts purchase include but are not limited to apparel, furniture, foodstuff, glassware, interior décor, jewelry and electronic gadgets such as mobile phones, television sets and computers.

Don't ever imagine that addiction to shopping is a problem that only affects the wealthy in society. This problem affects all age groups and both the low and high income earners. This means that you can be a shopping addict regardless of whether you are an average spender or filthy rich. Shopping addiction is not about how much money you spend. It is about whether you are making the right decision to purchase a given product.

Addiction to shopping starts gradually but at the end of it you'll be so much addicted that you'd rather borrow money than stop shopping. When completely addicted to shopping, you'll reach a point where you'll no longer be able to save some cash. All that you'll do is spend all the money you have and then start thinking of the consequences later. Therefore it is quite important that you find a way to stop this problem as soon as possible.

How Do You Know if You Are a Shopping Addict?

Even though there are numerous people addicted to shopping, very few of them know that they have this problem. There are several behaviors that distinguish shopping addicts.

Have you ever purchased something and then later realized that you could have saved more money if you had bought it elsewhere? For instance, you could have bought a mobile phone at $150 and then later realized that other outlets are selling the same phone at $125. Well, you are probably a shopping addict if you bought something at a higher price than the average market rates. Normally, shopping addicts tend to buy goods without sampling the entire market. By sampling the average market rates, you can save a huge portion of your money.

(a collection of mobile phones on display)

How many things of the same kind do you have at your home of office? For example, how many mobile phones do you have? Do you own several cars but rarely drive most of them? How many pairs of shoes do you have in your closet? How many pens do you have at your workplace? If you have more than one thing of the same kind in your home or office, then you are probably a shopping addict. Most of the people who are addicted to shopping purchase goods without thinking of the similar goods at their homes or offices. In a shopping addict's home, you can find several TV sets, mobile phones and even cars. The only limiting factor in shopping addicts is their total monthly/annual income.

Is there something in your home that you have never used since you bought it? When purchasing goods, shopping addicts never consider whether they need it. They just purchase something that they like or they've just seen being advertised. They therefore end up with a lot of expensive junk in their homes and offices. To be sure that you are not a shopping addict, just go through the stuff in your home and analyze each item. If you frequently use all the items in your home, then you are not a shopping addict. However, if there is something that you have never used for maybe five years, then you need help because you are a shopping addict.

Can you be able to account for all the money you earn? To perfectly answer this question, create a list of your expenses for the past one month. Make sure that you've included even the cash that you consider to be petty? Is the sum of the monthly expenses equal to your monthly income/earnings? If the monthly expenditure is equal to your income, then you have nothing to worry about. Just ensure that you cut on the unnecessary expenses and save the money. If your monthly expenditure is less than your earnings, you are headed in the right direction because it means that you are saving a portion of your income. However, if your monthly expenditure is more than your earnings, you need help because you are probably a shopping addict. The only way you can spend more than you are earning is by borrowing money from friends, family or even financial institutions.

How much debt do you have? How did you spend the cash you borrowed? Did you invest the money or did you buy unnecessary stuff? Having huge debts is a sign that you are a shopping addict. However, if you took a loan or borrowed money for investment purposes, then you are not a shopping addict. Most shopping addicts borrow money but use it to purchase useless/unnecessary gadgets/goods.

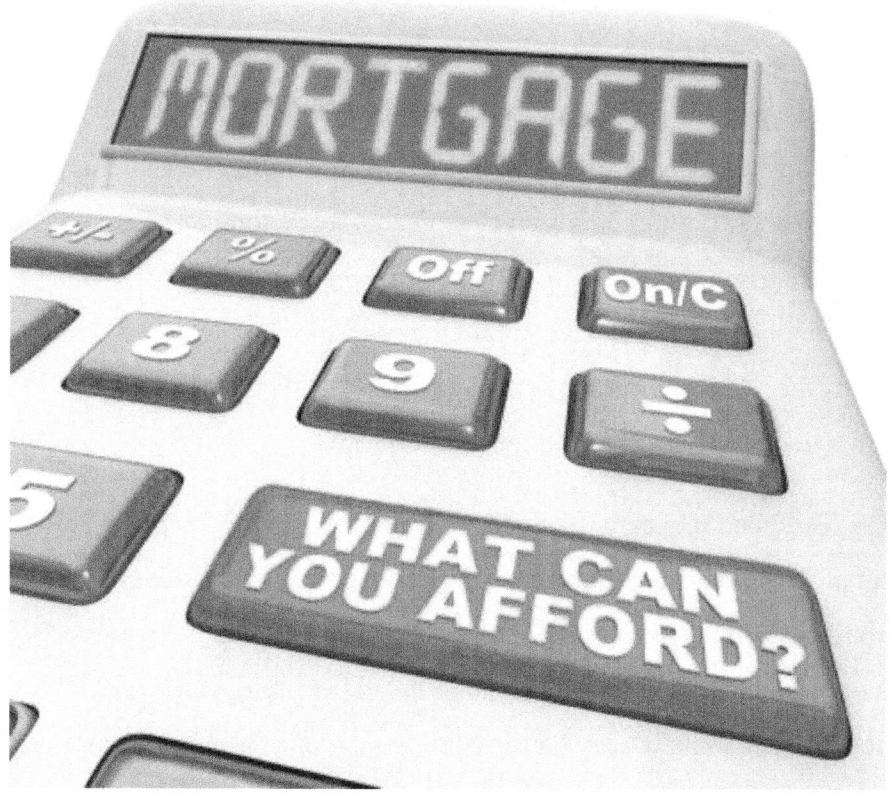

(mortgage calculator)

Can you afford your lifestyle? What percentage of money do you save each month? You are headed in the right direction if you can comfortably pay all your fixed monthly bills including mortgage or house rent, utility bills and meals. On the other hand, you could be a shopping addict if you always find yourself borrowing money from friends or financial institutions before the end of the month. You are headed in the right direction if you spend a very small portion of your earnings each month.

When was the last time you compared prices at different stores before making a purchase? Most of the people with shopping addiction problem tend to overspend money when purchasing products. They never bother to sample different outlets before settling on the most affordable retailer. Apart from overspending, shopping addicts tend to stick to one retailer for several months or even years. How will you know the average prices at other outlets if you always shop at the same department store or online marketplace?

Do you spend money without consulting other affected parties? How often do you consult your partner before purchasing anything? Do you occasionally spend other people's money without their consent? You need help on how to stop shopping addiction if you always find yourself spending money entrusted to you by other people. Shopping addicts have insatiable desire to spend money without considering the consequences of spending the cash. As long as they have money in the pocket, they can purchase anything at any time.

When going out with your partner, friends or even alone, how often do you come back home empty handed? Shopping addicts lack one simple but very critical skill-self-control. Some people are so much addicted to shopping that they never walk around empty handed. They will just buy anything on their way back home. If you realized that you never walk in to your home empty-handed, you are probably a shopping addict.

Do your friends and/or family members think you are a shopping addict? You can easily know if you are a shopping addict by asking them. If they think you like to spend too much, you should probably go ahead and seek help on how to overcome shopping addiction.

How consistent are you when it comes to monthly expenditure? Do your expenses vary depending on how much you've earned in a particular month? Have you noticed that you started spending more cash since your income increased? Inconsistency in monthly expenses is an indicator that you have a shopping addiction problem.

When you get some money that you were not expecting, what comes to your mind? Suppose you were to get $1000 today, what would you do with it? Would you go shopping? If yes, then you are a shopping addict and need help.

How Shopping Addiction is affecting Your Life Negatively

Just like any other type of addiction, shopping addiction is a serious problem that needs to be addressed as soon as possible. Apart from negatively affecting your life, addiction to shopping will affect all those close to you including your spouse, children and colleagues. At the national level, shopping addiction has a huge impact on the country's economic growth. Just ask yourself, how can the entire country grow economically if all or most of its citizens spend their cash on unnecessary/useless gadgets/goods? Shopping addiction also affects a company's output. If you are addicted to shopping, you'll be wasting so much time in malls and department stores instead of working. While at work, you'll waste time browsing merchant websites so as to know what to purchase.

(an underperforming employee)

Have you ever come across a colleague or family member who is always pestering everybody by borrowing money and never bothering to pay back in time? Do you still respect such a person? Well, one of the negative effects of shopping addiction is that you will lose respect from friends, workmates and family members. This is because you'll be frequently bothering them by borrowing money that you cannot afford to refund in time. Regardless of your profession or position in the company, you must never taint your image. Do something about your shopping addiction problem so as to earn the respect that you once had before you became an addict.

Shopping addiction can also lead to depression and other types of addiction including addiction to drugs and controlled substances. Shopping addicts find it quite hard to cope with life without money. They therefore get depressed whenever they've exhausted all the cash they have. Some shopping addicts even go to the extent of committing suicide simply because they lack money to spend on unimportant gadgets. Do something about your shopping addiction problem before getting into depression.

Have you ever tried to envision your future for the next couple of months? How do you see your financial stability in future? When addicted to shopping, you will never save enough money to safeguard your financial status in future. This means that you are likely to be bankrupt if you get fired or when you retire. You will even fail to afford medical insurance or your kid's school fees.

Shopping addiction can also lead to poor health and chronic diseases. When addicted to purchasing foodstuff, you will end up overeating every now and then. The frequency at which you eat will also increase. You're therefore likely to face conditions such as obesity. This will in turn result in poor health and reduced body immunity.

(your property might be repossessed or auctioned by financial institutions)

Have you ever dealt with auctioneers? If you are a shopping addict, your property can end up being auctioned by financial institutions or loan sharks. This is because you will find it hard to service loans. All the money that you earn will be spent on gadgets/goods that you won't ever need or use.

If you don't do something about your shopping addiction problem, your home will eventually be congested with unnecessary stuff. This means that there will be very little room for you to move around or for your kids to play. The probability of being injured is also slightly higher in small and congested homes than in large and spacious ones. To minimize chances of getting physical injuries while at home, ensure that you get rid of your shopping addiction problem.

Your personal life (relationship with members of the opposite sex) will also be affected if you are a shopping addict. Just ask yourself, can you date somebody with a shopping addiction problem? In order to have normal relationships you need to do something about your shopping addiction problem. If you are the sole breadwinner in your home, your spouse can easily leave you if you are a shopping addict. This is because you won't be able to take care of your family's financial needs.

Supposing you are the manager in a business entity, can you continue tolerating an employee who wastes company resources? If you are a shopping addict, you are likely to spend/waste company resources. This means that you risk being fired. You will also never get a promotion if you're a huge spender or shopping addict.

What Can You Do to Overcome Addiction to shopping?

There are several stages that people go through before they can get rid of their shopping addiction problem. People with this problem go through a denial stage. During this stage, they never acknowledge that they have a problem and need help. However, after some time they will come to terms with the fact that they are shopping addicts and hence seek help. After getting help and stopping the shopping addiction, they enter a phase in which they have to avoid getting back to the problem.

(use a shopping list)

The first and simplest way to get rid of your shopping addiction is have a sound budgetary plan. A budget is a list of all the things you need to buy and how much each one of them costs. When creating your monthly budget, you should start by listing the fixed costs (i.e. utility bills, medical insurance, house rent/mortgage etc.) You should then go ahead and list the variable costs (e.g. apparel, foodstuff, entertainment etc.) After creating the budget, you should review it and ensure that you've included everything that you'll need for a whole month. Also remember to set aside some cash for miscellaneous expenditure. If possible adjust the budget by removing all the items that you don't need. You can save the cash and invest it elsewhere. When creating your monthly budget, it is very important that you be realistic. Don't ever imagine that you can save your entire monthly income. You should therefore create a budget that is easy to implement. Apart from just creating a budget, you must ensure that you stick to the budget. You will have wasted your time creating a budget if you end up spending your money on something that is not in the budget.

Before purchasing any product, you should compare the average market prices at different outlets/retailers. Shopping addicts normally purchase products, in impulse and without bothering to know how much it costs to buy the same products elsewhere. So as to get rid of your shopping addiction problem, always try to sample the average market prices before purchasing anything.

If you are keen on stopping your shopping addiction problem, it is quite important that you live a life that you can afford. For example, why would you buy a car that consumes more fuel than you can afford each day. You won't utilize the car to its full potential. This rule also applies to all other commodities including your own home. Never take a mortgage that you can't afford to comfortably service. In order to stop your shopping addiction problem, you should nurture the culture of living a life that you can comfortably afford.

Before you purchase any product, try to think of the consequences of purchasing that particular product. For instance, if you buy a TV set worth $300, will you be able to take care of your daily expenditure. If yes, you can go ahead and buy the TV. However, you should not buy the TV if you won't be able to spend normally. By simply thinking of how shopping addiction will affect your life in the long-run and short-run, you can stop purchasing products anyhow.

(listen to music whenever you have the urge to purchase something)

You can also stop your addiction to shopping by ensuring that you are always busy doing something constructive. You can easily get tempted to go shopping once you're too idle. If you see and like something in a mall or the department store, don't just buy it. Find something to distract you so that you won't have the urge to purchase it. For example, you can call someone or start listening to music in your phone. You'll be preoccupying your mind with something else so that you don't think of shopping.

Suppose you saved half of your income, how much money would you have in maybe two years? If you imagine of all the money you'll be having if you stop unjustified spending, you can get rid of your shopping addiction problem. Whenever you feel like buying something, try thinking of all the money you'll have if you save the equivalent money for maybe 1 year.

Before buying anything, ask yourself, do you need it? If you can comfortably survive and perform all your duties and responsibilities without it, then you probably don't need it. By getting rid of all the expenses related to stuff that you don't need, you can get rid of your shopping addiction problem. Just ensure that you nurture the culture of spending cash on goods that you need only. However, this does not mean that you should deny yourself entertainment and relaxation money. After working so hard for several days or weeks, you need to go out, relax and have fun for some time. This way you'll regain your energy and increase your performance while at work. The best thing to do is allocate a given portion of your income to relaxation and entertainment. You should also make sure that you never exceed the money you allocated for this purpose.

Most addicts purchase goods spontaneously for as long as they have money with them. You can therefore stop your shopping addiction problem by ensuring that you never walk around with money that you are not planning to use. This way you won't spend money even if you have the urge to purchase something. When going out for a walk, plan in advance and know how much you'll need. You should also nurture the culture of planning your day very early in the morning. After planning your day, you'll know how much money you need for the entire day. You should then go ahead and carry the required money plus some extra emergency cash. However, the emergency money should only be used in case of an emergency.

You can also get rid of your shopping addiction problem by investing all your monthly savings. For instance, you can ensure that you purchase shares in the stock exchange using all the money that you won't need for a given month. This way you'll have no more than the cash you need. There is absolutely no way that you can spend money that you don't have. By investing your money, you'll basically be 'locking' the money and can't use it unless you sell your shares.

An experienced and dedicated financial adviser/consultant can also help you overcome your shopping addiction problem. If you've tried but haven't succeeded in stopping your shopping addiction problem, you should consider scheduling an appointment with a financial expert. Before purchasing any product, imagine you are the financial expert, would you advise somebody else to purchase it? There are countless financial experts that you can visit in the United States as well as in all the other parts of the world.

After discovering that you are a shopping addict, make sure that your family and friends know that you have the problem. This way they can do something to help you out. Whenever going out, make sure that you're never alone. Always walk in the company of a friend or family member who knows that you have a shopping addiction problem.This way he/she will try to stop you from purchasing something that you don't need or had not budgeted for. If possible ensure that the friend or family member is the one carrying all the money. He/she will then give you the money that you need when you need it and only if you've justified its usage. .

Having a financial mentor is the best thing that you can ever do. A mentor is somebody you'll be looking up to whenever you have the urge to go spending. When choosing a mentor, look for somebody who has managed to come out of a shopping addiction problem. The perfect example of a mentor is Sir Richard Branson(British)-the owner of Virgin group of companies. He was once a truck driver but he is currently a billionaire who owns several planes, high-end hotels and other businesses. By simply thinking of how much he had to save so as to invest in his businesses, you can easily stop your shopping addiction problem. Find a similar mentor near your home and look up to him. Before purchasing anything, just imagine you are him/her- would you purchase the good.

Avoid asking for money from friends or even financial institutions. You should only borrow money when you need to invest in something on in an emergency. If you borrow money that you don't need, you will end up purchasing something that you won't ever use or need. If possible, ask your friends and family to promise you that they won't ever loan you money unless you need it.

Some people celebrate milestones and important achievements in life by going on a shopping spree and spending huge sums of money. If you're keen on getting rid of your shopping addiction problem, you have to find better ways of celebrating important milestones and achievements in your life. For instance, you can decide to go on holiday instead of going on a shopping spree after achieving a given goal.

Always insist on purchasing original and high quality products so as to stop your shopping addiction problem. Counterfeit and low quality products have a short lifespan and therefore the user has to frequently replace them. By always purchasing such products, you'll be forced to go shopping frequently or as soon as the gadget malfunctions. You'll therefore get used to buying the gadget that you'll end up becoming a shopping addict.

How to Ensure You Won't Ever Become a Shopping Addict Again

After getting rid of your shopping addiction problem, you have to make sure that you won't ever become an addict. You would have wasted so much time if you start spending money anyhow after working so hard to stop your shopping addiction. So as never to go back to shopping addiction you need to totally transform your lifestyle, embrace good virtues and learn to take responsibility for your own life.

(avoid window shopping)

Never go shopping without a shopping list. When going to replenish the stuff in your home, you should first create a shopping list. If you start shopping without the list, you might end up buying something that you had not planned for. You might also buy something that you already have. If you have a habit of purchasing goods without a shopping list, you need to stop it immediately because you'll end up being a shopping addict.

Window-shopping should be avoided especially if you have some cash lying somewhere. By simply looking at a product on display, you might end up purchasing it if you have some money somewhere. If you stop window-shopping you can rest assured that you won't ever become a shopping addict again.

Apart from avoiding window-shopping, you should avoid visiting online marketplaces including eBay.com and Amazon.com. Online merchants know how to market their products and how to convince you to purchase the products. They hype their products and occasionally trick potential customers to purchase the products on sale. By simply visiting a merchant website, you can be tempted to purchase a product being advertised. So as to ensure that you won't ever become a shopping addict, never visit such websites unless you need something specific.

Suppose you get fired today, will your lifestyle change for the worse? If yes, you need to think about it and hence invest in your future. By simply thinking of the uncertainties in your future, you will never go back to shopping addiction. This is because you'll be saving all your extra income so as to safeguard the future.

Have you ever thought of the fact that you are enriching somebody simply because you are a shopping addict? Imagine of all the money you'll spend in a given store if you go shopping there. You can become a richer person if you save the money that you could have used. Whenever you're tempted to spend money on something, ask yourself this question; why enrich other people instead of enriching yourself?

By selling all the stuff that you don't need, you can ensure that you never fall back to your shopping addiction problem. Why would you want to purchase something that you sold a few days or weeks ago? If you simply sell the unnecessary products in your home, you can be sure that you won't ever buy them again.

Set specific financial goals in your life and strive to achieve them. Whenever you have a given financial goal, you will save all your extra money, until you have achieved it. For instance, you can decide to save a minimum of $5000 within 3 months. For as long as you have not achieved that objective, you won't be tempted to go shopping. This means that you will never go back to shopping addiction if you come up with a new objective after achieving the previous one.

Making payments online, through debit cards or credit cards gives buyers an illusion that they are not spending money. They therefore tend to spend more money than they could have spent if they were paying in cash. You can ensure that you won't ever become an addict by always paying in cash.

Conclusion

Now that you know how to know if you are a shopping addict and what to do so as to get rid of the problem, you just need to know what to do with the money that you will save. Investing the money in a profit making business is one of the best ways to use the cash.

With careful implementation of the tips in this book, you can transform your life completely. You can also use the tips in this book to help a friend or relative with shopping addiction problem.

When trying to get rid of your shopping addiction, always remember that you are not the only one having the problem. You should therefore never give up in your quest to get rid of the problem. Persevere and believe in yourself. If other people have managed to stop shopping addiction, why can't you also manage to do it?

Author Bio

Colvin Tonya Nyakundi is a freelance writer and co-author of 'Simple Steps to Help You Overcome Shopping Addiction.' Apart from that book, he has a portfolio of several other publications accumulated in the more than two years that he has been freelancing through www.odesk.com.

He has authored several personal relationships, construction and real estate, lifestyle and travel and holiday guide publications. Other books that he has co-authored include 'How to Survive in the Woods', 'How to Start Making Money Online', 'How to Survive in a Desert', 'How to Improve Your Communication Skills,' 'Construction Guide for New Investors in Real Estate,' 'How to Make Your Backyard a Magnificent Venue for Hosting Events', 'How to Identify the Perfect Holiday Destination', "How Your Favorite Meal Could be Killing You Slowly" and 'How to Prepare and Survive in a Foreign Country.' You can get in touch with him through his official Facebook account, tonyanc@facebook.com.

Check out some of the other JD-Biz Publishing books

[Gardening Series on Amazon](#)

Health Learning Series

Simple Steps to Help You Overcome Shopping Addiction   Page 32

Country Life Books

Simple Steps to Help You Overcome Shopping Addiction   Page 34

Health Learning Series

Amazing Animal Book Series

Learn To Draw Series

How to Build and Plan Books

Simple Steps to Help You Overcome Shopping Addiction   Page 38

Entrepreneur Book Series

Our books are available at

1. Amazon.com
2. Barnes and Noble
3. Itunes
4. Kobo
5. Smashwords
6. Google Play Books

Publisher

JD-Biz Corp
P O Box 374
Mendon, Utah 84325
http://www.jd-biz.com/

Printed in Great Britain
by Amazon